Armed Gunmen, True Facts, and Other Ridiculous Nonsense

Armed Gunmen, True Facts, and Other Ridiculous Nonsense

A COMPILED COMPENDIUM OF
REPETITIVE REDUNDANCIES

Richard Kallan

Pantheon Books, New York

Pantheon Books and colophon are registered trademarks
of Random House, Inc.

Library of Congress Cataloging-in-Publication Data
Kallan, Richard A., [date]
Armed gunmen, true facts, and other ridiculous nonsense : a
compiled compendium of repetitive redundancies / Richard Kallan.
p. cm.
Includes index.
ISBN 0-375-42352-4
1. English language—Errors of usage.   2. Pleonasm.   I. Title.
PE1460.K36 2005
428—dc22   2004065017

www.pantheonbooks.com
Printed in the United States of America
First Edition
9 8 7 6 5 4 3 2 1

For Darla,
whose repetitive acts of kindness
represent the best of all
redundancies

❧ Contents ❧

✿ Introduction ✿

A rmed *gunmen,* true *facts,* and other *ridiculous nonsense.* All are tautologies—their modifying language essentially repeats the meaning of the word being modified.

Tautology (from the Greek *tautologia: tauto,* the same; *logia,* to speak) is a common form of redundancy not to be confused with pleonasm or circumlocution. Pleonasm, or the use of more words than required, is characterized by unnecessary, rather than repetitive, verbiage. [There exist] many sentences [that could serve to] illustrate [the occurrence of] pleonasm, but because [of the fact that] space is limited and [in order] to save time, this will [have to] do. Circumlocution is also characterized by wordiness, but it best describes indirect, roundabout constructions: "I am of the personal opinion" ("I think"); or "They are of the Hindu persuasion" ("They are Hindus").

Deliberate use of tautologies in speech can provide a certain catharsis: "The stupid-idiotic-dumb plumber never showed up!" Although rarely acceptable in written form, oral tautologies can emphasize ideas and underscore meaning.

Admittedly, several word combinations that technically qualify as tautologies, such as *good Samaritan, positive assurance,* and *overabundance,* have become so popular that their prefacing adjectives or prefixes are no longer considered modifiers; instead, they are seen as integral parts of compound nouns, in much the same way that certain adjectives help form compounds such as *upper class, short story,* and *Big Brother.*

Similarly, many figures of speech would lose their impact if they were truncated. *Aid and abet, above and beyond, betwixt and between, bits and pieces, bound and determined, cease and desist, dead and gone, first and foremost, forever and ever, null and void, pick and choose, rant and rave,* and *rules and regulations* offer rhythmic force as well as ironic emphasis in their redundancies.

More often, however, the use of tautologies is unintentional and problematic. The excess word or phrase tends to weigh down the text and slow the reader. Too, it may cloud what is meant. *Mental telepathy, planned conspiracies,* and *small dwarfs,* for example, convey the possibility of physical telepathy, spontaneous conspiracies, and giant dwarfs. Such inadvertent comic constructions undermine the writer's authority.

This book offers an antidote by whimsically cataloging our most popular tautologies. It is not intended to be an exhaustive investigation; even the lists of "close relatives" that accompany many of the entries are selective. Nor do I dwell on the many contexts that might legitimize certain tautologies. And, of course, I could not possibly capture every new tautology.

To be sure, any book about language is an evolving project. For now, the goal is to alert readers to our propensity for tautology—to present a *compiled compendium* of *repetitive redundancies* so that readers can *see with their own two eyes* how to *remove and eliminate* such *excessive verbiage* from their *communicative language.*

🕊

Double Trouble

Abnormally Strange

Stranger than ho-hum, everyday normal strange.

CLOSE RELATIVE
oddly peculiar

Deliberate Lie

More forthright than the inadvertent lie.

CLOSE RELATIVES
deceitful lie
deceptive lie
misleading lie

Hidden Pitfall

A pitfall unannounced by bells and whistles.

Poisonous Venom

Once bitten, twice dead.

CLOSE RELATIVE
toxic poison

False Pretense

The worst kind of pretense, i.e., it's not even true.

CLOSE RELATIVES
false fabrication
. . . facade
  front
  illusion
  misrepresentation

Negative Stigma

What you get when you subtract three stigmas from two.

CLOSE RELATIVES
negative notoriety
public notoriety

Armed Gunman

When you need to distinguish between two gunmen,
one of whom is missing a couple of limbs.

Electrical Voltage

Caution: shocking language!

Crazy Lunatic

Not a candidate for group therapy.

Missing Gaps

Gaps that vanish without a trace.

Drunken Sot

A sot committed to leaving a *memorable impression*.

Violent Explosion

Gentle explosion's evil twin.

Stupid Idiot

Often found in the company of the *moronic jerk* and the *idiotic moron*.

Disorganized Mess

A mess that's poorly designed and engineered.

CLOSE RELATIVES
  filthy dirty
  scrubbed clean

Extreme Fanatic

One who is repulsed by moderate fanaticism.

Advance Warning

A warning after the fact is an "I told you so."

CLOSE RELATIVES

advance or prior arrangement
. . . consent
    forecast
    notice
    planning
    preparation
    reservation
    scouting
forecast ahead
forewarn
plan ahead
prefrozen
prenotify
prepare in advance
preplan
prewarn
prewrap

project ahead
projected forecast
reserve ahead
warn ahead

Convicted Felon

Once convicted, the felon stands alone.

CLOSE RELATIVE

prison convict

Dangerous Lightning

Lightning with a dark side.

Face-to-Face Confrontation

An encounter you can't turn your back on.

Hired Mercenary

More expensive than your average, pro bono hired gun.

CLOSE RELATIVE

paid prostitute

Attacked by Assailant

Why can't assailants be more loving?

Bad Vices

Vices lacking virtues.

CLOSE RELATIVE

good virtues

Forcible Rape

When permission to rape isn't granted.

Past Overdue

A past not worth mentioning.

Overused Cliché

A familiarity that breeds contempt.

CLOSE RELATIVE

trite cliché

Pathological Disease

A diseased disease.

Deadly Killer

A killer who's serious.

CLOSE RELATIVES

dead body
dead corpse

Planned Conspiracy

A conspiracy devoid of spontaneity.

Hostile Antagonist

One who doesn't bring flowers or chocolate.

CLOSE RELATIVE

polar opposite

Long Chronic Illness

Nothing like your normal twenty-four-hour chronic illness.

CLOSE RELATIVE

long litany

Monetary Fine

When you want to ensure that payment isn't made with three chickens and a goat.

CLOSE RELATIVE

monetary funding

Stern Dutch Uncle

Stricter than a laid-back Dutch uncle.

CLOSE RELATIVE
strict disciplinarian

Ridiculous Nonsense

Nonsense unencumbered by thoughtful analysis.

Odorous Smell

The calling card of a real stinker.

CLOSE RELATIVES

offensive stench
sweet fragrance

Self-Confessed

Only Houdini could confess for someone else.

CLOSE RELATIVE

self-portrait of myself

Weird Freak

The counterpart to the ordinary freak.

Wild Savage

A savage who lacks civility.

CLOSE RELATIVE

uncivilized barbarian

Serious Crisis

Not to be confused with all those whimsical crises.

CLOSE RELATIVE

vital necessity

Terrible Tragedy

A tragedy that's no laughing matter.

Tough Challenge

A challenge from the wrong side of the tracks.

CLOSE RELATIVES

adverse obstacle
difficult dilemma

Strangle to Death

Overkill.

CLOSE RELATIVES

decapitate the head
fatally electrocute
suffocate to death

Unsolved Problem

More problematic than a solved problem.

CLOSE RELATIVE

unsolved mystery

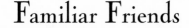

Familiar Friends

☛ Hopeful Optimist

Down with all those pessimistic optimists!

Black Crow

The outcast in those large albino flocks.

CLOSE RELATIVES

red robin
spotted leopard

General Public

A public worthy of salute.

Royal Prince

Snooty foe of the proletariat prince.

CLOSE RELATIVES

royal highness
. . . king
princess
queen

Qualified Expert

Nemesis of the know-nothing expert.

CLOSE RELATIVES

skilled or trained craftsman
. . . expert
professional

Brand-New Beginner

A beginner who's not a *seasoned veteran*.

CLOSE RELATIVES

first-time beginner
fresh beginner
new recruit
raw recruit

Dumb Mute

A mute who has nothing to say anyway.

Invited Guest

A fine, upstanding tautology that sometimes slums with its lowlife oxymoronic cousin—the uninvited guest.

CLOSE RELATIVE

uninvited intruder

❧ Original Founder

Forerunner to the second founder.

CLOSE RELATIVES

first ever
first or originally began
. . . coined
   conceived
   created
   debuted
   discovered
   established
   founded
   introduced
   invented
   originated
   revealed
   started
   uncovered
   unveiled
first prototype

Fellow Colleague

An ally in the fight against fellow enemies.

CLOSE RELATIVES

fellow classmate
fellow peer

Personal Friend

A friend you actually know.

CLOSE RELATIVES

my own personal
my personal opinion

Jewish Rabbi

More authentic than a Catholic rabbi.

Single Bachelor

Aka a free-range chicken.

CLOSE RELATIVES

single entity
single one
unmarried bachelor

Funny Comic

One who's employed.

humorous joke

Innocent Bystander

A bystander inexperienced in the ways of the world.

Present Incumbent

Incumbency is present even when the incumbent isn't.

at the present moment

Singing Duet

A duet that's more than just talk.

Wise Sage

The sage's sage.

Wealthy Millionaire

Like really, really rich.

CLOSE RELATIVES

indigent poor
wealthy philanthropist

Small Dwarf

The large ones can be found in their *native habitat* along
with *huge throngs* of *tall giants* and *giant titans*. But the little
ones, some say, reside in *underground subways* beneath *tall
skyscrapers* owned by *huge conglomerates*.

little, small, or tiny bit
. . . detail
    fraction⋆
    particle
    smidgen
    speck
    trace
microscopic bacteria
residual trace

⋆Technically, of course, a fraction can be a large percentage,
like seven-eighths.

Surviving Widow

The last one standing in an all-widow game of
Russian roulette.

CLOSE RELATIVE

widow of the late

Unknown Stranger

A stranger without a name tag.

CLOSE RELATIVE

anonymous stranger

Young Infant

An infant not yet mature and sophisticated.

CLOSE RELATIVES

young adolescent
. . . baby
juvenile
lad

Famous Celebrity

A celebrity who no longer enjoys anonymity.

CLOSE RELATIVES

big V.I.P.
notable luminary

Stage Directions,
Take Two

Disappear from View

The scenic way to disappear.

CLOSE RELATIVES
disappear from sight
erode away
fade away

Laugh Out Loud

The most outspoken way of laughing.

CLOSE RELATIVE
talk out loud

Clap with Both Hands

But not with all three.

Ascend Up · Fall Down

Ultimate gymnastics: ascending down and falling up.

CLOSE RELATIVES

bubble up
build up
climb up
fill up
hoist up
lift up
pile up
raise up
rise up
stand up

condense down
descend down

drink down
drop down
dwindle down
kneel down
melt down
narrow down
pare down
plummet down
plunge down
pour down
reduce down
shrink down
sink down
sit down*
slip down
swallow down
swoop down
trickle down

*We sit *down*, although we sometimes ask the
posture-imperfect to sit *up*.

Full Stop

An unabridged stop.

Repeat Again

An encore presentation.

CLOSE RELATIVES

recur again
recur over and over
recurring motif
recurring pattern
reiterate again
repeat over
repetitive motif
repetitive pattern
restate again
resume again
reuse again
revive again

Follow After

When you're tired of following before.

CLOSE RELATIVES

follow behind
leave behind
trail behind

Advance Forward

As distinguished from advancing backward.

CLOSE RELATIVES

advance forth
advance onward
forward progress
leap forward
proceed forth
proceed onward

Sink to the Ground

As if sinking allowed for directional options.

CLOSE RELATIVES

raze to the ground
sink to the bottom

Weave In and Out

A unique method of weaving.

CLOSE RELATIVE

interweave

Subtle Nuance

A nuance that's not *blatantly obvious*.

CLOSE RELATIVES

patently clear
readily apparent

Enter In

Easier than entering out.

CLOSE RELATIVE

in between

Traverse Across

CIA code for double-crossed.

CLOSE RELATIVES

> cover over
> flood over
> skip over
> spill over
> traverse over

Surround on All Sides

The most confining of surroundings.

CLOSE RELATIVES

surrounding circumstances
surrounding environment

Return Back

Simpler than returning forward.

CLOSE RELATIVES

loop back
rebound back
recede back
recoil back
reflect back
remand back
remit back
repay back
reply back
respond back
restore back
retreat back
revert back
trace back

Quick Dash

Shorter than a long-distance dash.

CLOSE RELATIVES

expedite quickly
flee quickly
skim quickly
speed racer

Circle Around

When circling square won't do.

Soft Whisper

A popular alternative to the screaming whisper.

Stumble Accidentally

To stumble without rehearsal.

Places and Times
Revisited

(Six) A.M. in the Morning

Earlier than the *noontime* that arrives at twelve.

Perfect Utopia

Better than a run-down Utopia.

All Throughout

More pervasive than occasionally throughout.

CLOSE RELATIVES

permeating the entire
permeating throughout
pervading the whole
pervading throughout
throughout the duration of
throughout the entire

Past History

History that's already happened.

CLOSE RELATIVES

historical past
. . . precedent
    record
never before
. . . before in the past
    ever

past or previous accomplishment
. . . achievement
   deed
   experience
   memory

Intersection of Hollywood and Vine

An intersection crowded by two words too many.

Rural Countryside

Home to the *rural farm*.

Left-Hand Side · Right-Hand Side

Helping hands not needed.

Easter Sunday

Holier—and more convenient—than an Easter Wednesday.

Close Proximity

Nearer than distant proximity.

Safe Sanctuary

Unlike those fly-by-night sanctuaries.

Raining Outside

Less surprising than when it rains inside.

CLOSE RELATIVES

hailing outside
snowing outside
sunny outside
windy outside

Future Expectations

Expectations unachieved in advance.

CLOSE RELATIVES

future plans*
future prospect

*Plans may be immediate or long-range,
but they always describe the future.

Sick Leave Time

When you need twice the time to heal.

CLOSE RELATIVES

together at the same time
until the time
until the time when
while at the same time

Matinee Performance

A matinee that requires no performance.

Undisclosed Secret Location

More clandestine than a disclosed secret location.

Immediately Adjoining

Closer than that which eventually adjoins.

CLOSE RELATIVE
closely adjoining

Scheduled Appointment

Surest way to discourage impromptu appointments.

CLOSE RELATIVE
time schedule

Eventually Inevitable

Inevitability you can bet on.

Today's Soup du Jour

Fresher than yesterday's soup du jour.

Up in the Sky

Up isn't needed unless Chicken Little is right.

CLOSE RELATIVES

down in the basement
out in the open
up in the attic
up on the roof

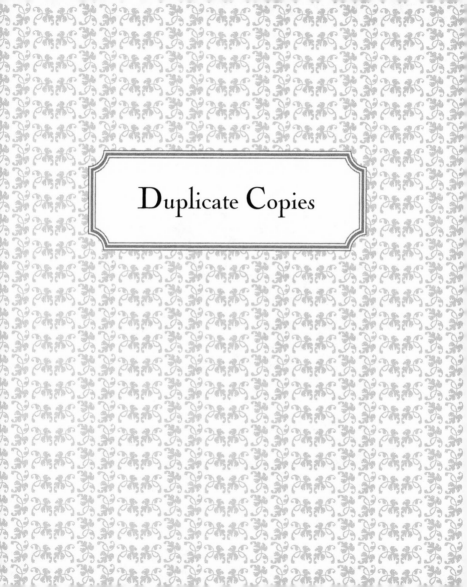

Duplicate Copies

Alternative Choice

When choice has an understudy.

CLOSE RELATIVES

optional accessory
optional choice

Core Essence

The soul that lurks beneath surface essence.

CLOSE RELATIVE

essential core

Each and Every

When you want to cover all your bases, twice.

complete and utter
factual and accurate
fair and equitable
full and complete
long and protracted
mix and mingle
neat and tidy
optimize and maximize
over and above
over and done
recycled and used again
separate and discrete
shape and form
true and accurate
uses and applications
various and sundry
yell and scream

May Perhaps

When a simple *may* or *perhaps* would be too
bold a commitment.

may possibly
may potentially
maybe, maybe not
might perhaps
. . . possibly
    potentially

Approximately Around

Doubly unsure.

estimated at about

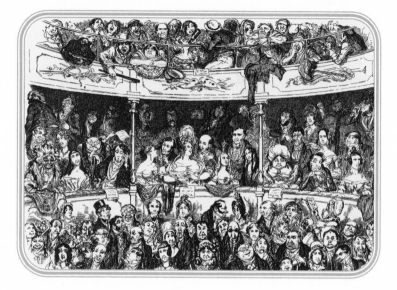

Maximum Limit

Midway between your initial limit and your absolute limit.

CLOSE RELATIVE

ultimate limit

Necessary Prerequisite

When mandatory compliance isn't optional.

basic essentials
basic fundamentals
essential necessity
essential prerequisite
important essentials
important fundamentals
necessary essentials
necessary fundamentals
required prerequisite

Adequate Enough

Adequate would be enough and *enough*
would be adequate.

sufficient enough

Sum Total

The only time you can cut the sum or total
without the numbers changing.

CLOSE RELATIVES

end product
end result

Fortunate Luck

More fortuitous than planned luck.

Well-Established Custom

Mentor to the newly invented custom.

CLOSE RELATIVES

well-established norm
. . . protocol
standard

track record
tradition
prescribed protocol
standard custom
usual custom

Component Part

Fail-safe strategy should a part
(or component) disappear.

Kiss-Kiss, Bye-Bye:
An Abbreviated Marriage
and Divorce Story

(They're) Both Alike

Word magic: delete *both* and they're still alike.

CLOSE RELATIVE

(they) both agreed

⬤ Shared Dialogue

More conversational than a shared monologue.

CLOSE RELATIVES

conversational dialogue
interactive dialogue
one-way monologue
two-way conversation

Exactly the Same

Sameness, *pure and unadulterated.*

CLOSE RELATIVES

exact duplicate
. . . equivalent
mirror image
exactly identical

Bouquet of Flowers

Too flowery.

CLOSE RELATIVE

flower boutonniere

The Bonafide Real Thing

What counterfeit reality can never be.

genuine sincerity
genuinely real

Married to Her Husband

The fate of a wedded wife.

biography of his life
married to his wife
own autobiography

Joint Partnership

A couple of potheads sharing dope.

CLOSE RELATIVES

joint agreement
. . . collaboration
cooperation
cosponsorship

Coequal

Equality taken to the next level.

CLOSE RELATIVES

bisect into two parts
commingle
equal halves (unless they come from different wholes)
pair of twins
two twins (unless they come from different parents)

Mutual Cooperation

Team version of solo cooperation.

CLOSE RELATIVES

mutual agreement
mutual friendship

Add Together

Adding *apart* would be a neat trick.

CLOSE RELATIVES

assemble together
attach together
blend together
bond together
bundle together
cluster together
cohabit together
collaborate together
combine together

congregate together
connect together
converge together
cooperate together
flock together
fuse together
huddle together
link together
merge together
mesh together
mingle together
mix together
weave together

Add an Additional

Better yet, subtract the last two (words).

CLOSE RELATIVES

added bonus
added perk
extra bonus

Families with Children

Ultrafamilial.

CLOSE RELATIVE

parents with children

Disclose for the First Time

Disclosures occur once, although titillating ones
may be repeated.

CLOSE RELATIVES

divulge for the first time
introduce for the first time
reveal for the first time

Honest Truth

When all other truths fail.

Carefully Scrutinize

When sloppy scrutiny won't do.

CLOSE RELATIVE

closely scrutinize

Unsubstantiated Allegation

An allegation that's not absolutely, positively true.

CLOSE RELATIVES

alleged suspect
unproven allegation
unsubstantiated rumor

Yell Loudly

Form of yelling favored by the hard of hearing.

bellow loudly
holler loudly
roar loudly
scream loudly
shout loudly
shriek loudly

More Superior

When superior isn't judgmental enough.

more inferior

Divided by a Partition

More divisive than being joined by a partition.

Whether or Not

Slow-moving due to added whether conditions.

(To) Separate Apart

Separating together would be a parting
worth remembering.

CLOSE RELATIVES

crumble apart
disintegrate into pieces
sever off

❧

Correspond Back and Forth

Guaranteed to get a *return response.*

CLOSE RELATIVES

commute back and forth
seesaw up and down
shuttle back and forth
vacillate back and forth
volley back and forth
waffle back and forth

Sworn Affidavit

An affidavit signed twice, usually with an
ink pen and a *lead pencil*.

And Etc. (and and so forth)

Question: What do you call two consecutive *ands*?
Answer: A well-coordinated redundancy.

CLOSE RELATIVES

so consequently
. . . hence
therefore
thus
yet however
yet nevertheless

Is the Current · Was the Former

Key to passing Grammar 101: remembering that the
present is and the past was.

Auction Sale

Where you go when you want to buy
an auction.

Endorse the Back

Banking rule #136:
to endorse means to sign on the back.

Cash Money

Spendable currency.

Mass Exodus

A super-sized exodus.

CLOSE RELATIVE

mass epidemic

Completely Finished

What follows almost totally done.

CLOSE RELATIVES
(a very limited list)

completely abolish
. . . annihilate
    certain
    consistent
    demolish
    destroy
    devoid
    eliminate
    empty
    equal
    eradicate
    full
    infinite (or any word whose *in-*
       or *im-* prefix denotes *not*)
    liquidate

lost

omnipotent (or any word with an *omni-* prefix)

pure

separate

sure

surround

unabridged (or any word with an *un-* prefix)

unanimous

unified

unique

worthless (or any word with a *-less* suffix)

Final End ☛

The final, no-kidding end that comes at the conclusion of all previous ends.

CLOSE RELATIVES

farewell swan song
final or ultimate climax
. . . completion
  conclusion
  end
  farewell
  outcome
  upshot
last farewell

Remaining Residue

New Innovation

Preferable to an old innovation.

CLOSE RELATIVES

new birth
. . . breakthrough
    change
    discovery
    initiative
    revelation
pioneer breakthrough

Clinging Vine

A needy variety of vine, usually in a codependent
relationship with a trellis.

Contributing Factor

Only nonfactors are noncontributing.

AC Current

Whoa! A double blast: alternating current current.

CLOSE RELATIVES

ABM missile
ABS brakes
ACT test
ATM machine
CAD design
CD ROM disk
CNN network
DC current
DL list
DMZ zone
DOS operating system
dot.com
DVD disk

ER room
HIV virus
ICU unit
IRA account
ISBN number
LCD display
LED diode
NATO organization
NT technology
OPEC nations
OR room
PC computer
PIN number
SALT talks
SAM missile
SAT test
SSN#
STD disease
UPC code
URL address
VAT tax
VIN number

Panacea for All Ills

An overachieving panacea.

Polite Euphemism

A euphemism too refined for the rough-and-tumble
world of euphemistic dialogue.

Bald-Headed

"Where else is that *handsome-looking, large-sized, circular-shaped* man bald?" she asked with a *wide-mouthed grin*—sheepishly aware that she was preoccupied with *physical appearance.*

Hot Water Heater

Stolen merchandise.

CLOSE RELATIVES

fiery conflagration
freezing ice
frozen tundra
hot boiling water
. . . molten metal
steam

Mental Telepathy

More cerebral than physical telepathy.

CLOSE RELATIVES

mental awareness
mentally insane
mulling over in my mind
thinking to myself

Still Persist

Another still that warrants prohibition.

CLOSE RELATIVES

constantly evolving
continue to persist
continue to remain
continuously without interruption
currently in progress
long enduring

Cancel Out

Yes, cancel *out*.

CLOSE RELATIVES

  block out
  eliminate out
  filter out
  leak out
  loan out

Irregardless

Product of the suffix-challenged.

CLOSE RELATIVES

  inflammable
  reconvert
  unloosen
  unpeel
  unshuck
  unthaw

Consensus of Opinion

Way too opinionated.

CLOSE RELATIVES

general consensus
popular consensus

Foreign Import

An import that hasn't been domesticated.

CLOSE RELATIVES

foreign-born immigrant
local neighbor
near neighbor

Empty Hole

A hole that's never experienced fulfillment.

CLOSE RELATIVES

empty vacuum
hollow tube
open cavity
open trench

Dressed in Clothes

Simply dressed is always best.

CLOSE RELATIVES

appreciate / depreciate in value
architecture of the building
attractive in appearance
audible to the ear
chronology of time
consecutive in a row
cubic feet in volume
curious in nature
earlier / later in time
few in number
heavy in weight
hours of time
knots per hour
landscape of the grounds
miles in distance
period of time
rate of speed

red in color
soft to the touch
square in shape
square miles of area
stunted in growth
ten dollars in cost
ten hours of time
visible to the eye
worthy of merit

Rank Order

Rank has its privileges: this one takes no orders.

Swinging Pendulum

Translation: the pendulum worked.

CLOSE RELATIVE

orbiting satellite

Three-Sided Triangle

Welcome to remedial math.

CLOSE RELATIVES

curved arc
perpendicular right angle

Simply Plain

When *plain* isn't plain enough.

Holy Bible

One with religious overtones.

CLOSE RELATIVE

sacred scripture

❧

Different Varieties

Without variation, varieties vary.

CLOSE RELATIVE

various varieties

Condensed Summary

A summary in which every other word is left out.

brief glance
. . . instant
moment
synopsis
fleeting instant
fleeting moment

Natural Instinct

The standard by which all artificially created instinct
is measured.

natural herbs
natural life

Either One

Generally independent, *either* needs no one.

CLOSE RELATIVES

either one or the other
neither one

Penetrate Into · Protrude Out

The only feat comparable to penetrating *out*
is protruding *in*.

CLOSE RELATIVES

emerge out
enter into
exit out
extend out
probe into
radiate out
spread out
stretch out

Foot Pedal

Look, Ma, I'm pedaling with no hands!

Old Antique

A sorry sight next to *modern state-of-the-art* antiques.

CLOSE RELATIVES

ancient fossil
. . . proverb
   relic
old adage
. . . classic
   cliché
   maxim
   proverb
   relic
relic from the past

Passing Fad

A fad that knows nothing of custom and tradition.

CLOSE RELATIVES

current fad
current trend

Glowing Ember

A romantically fulfilled ember.

With Au Jus

Pardon my French. More français French: *apropos for the
occasion, evening soiree, final adieu, good bon mot,
please RSVP, sudden coup d'état.*

·≫✦≪·

Temporary Loan

Permanent loans lead to temporary relationships.

borrowed loan
outstanding existing loan
temporary postponement
. . . reprieve
   stopgap

Free Gift

Finally: a gift for which you're not charged.

CLOSE RELATIVES

free giveaway
. . . of charge
pass

Photosensitive to Light

The most illuminating form of photosensitivity.

Positive Proton

A proton unaffected by the negativity of neighboring electrons.

CLOSE RELATIVES

negative cathode
negative electron
positive anode

Soothing Balm

A balm that achieves self-actualization.

CLOSE RELATIVES

soothing emollient
soothing salve

Written Document

Wordier than a nonverbal document.

CLOSE RELATIVE

written script

Sudden Impulse

Impulse that doesn't embrace a strategic plan.

CLOSE RELATIVES

spur-of-the-moment impulse
sudden crisis
. . . urge
    whim

Successfully Pass

When merely passing won't suffice.

CLOSE RELATIVE

successfully accomplish

Surface Polish

The most shallow of finishes.

Surprise Upset

Expected upset = losing gambler.

CLOSE RELATIVES

surprise pop quiz
unexpected emergency
unexpected surprise

Wooden Stick

The stick preferred by four out of five naturalists.

CLOSE RELATIVE

steel rebar

Visual Sight

A sight to see.

Up Until

Mercifully, *up* must be put down.

Surplus Left Over

What's left when a surplus sale isn't a total success.

A Concluding Coda
from the Author's Pen

Although at times I felt *isolated by myself,* writing this book has been the *realization of a dream come true.* As I *myself look back in retrospect,* I *personally* never gave up hope that it would someday be my *lasting legacy.* I envisioned *actively engaged* readers developing the *automatic habit* of using it *365 calendar days a year* as *part and parcel* of their *regular routine.*

I offer *grateful thanks* to *any and all* who helped me *classify into groups* and *organizationally structure* the book's *hundreds and hundreds* of tautologies so that I could *compare them to one another.* I especially want to acknowledge the *head honcho* of the *outdoor amphitheater,* where the *conceptual idea* for this work came to me as I sat watching the *morning sunrise* (or was it the *evening sunset?*) in the *fine mist* of a *damp fog.* While eating *breakfast cereal,* sipping *chowder soup,* and nibbling on a *tuna fish* sandwich and *cheese quesadilla* topped with a garnish of *shrimp scampi, salsa sauce,* and *sour lemon,* I thought about my *future ahead* and the prospect of gaining *hands-on experience*—and also about having an *ice cream sundae* for dessert.

As I *looked ahead to the future* and my next *vacation trip,* I was *suddenly startled* by an *emergency situation:* a woman, snorting *adhesive glue* and smoking some sort of *illegal contraband* that had been *illegally smuggled,* began screaming *deliberately on purpose* that she had *just recently* escaped from a *sadly tragic* life of *forced slavery* and *intimate sexual practices*; and that she now yearned for the *sparkling glitter* afforded by her *only other alternative:* becoming a *bare naked, nude topless* dancer at *Hawaiian luaus.* No longer could she *postpone until later* her dream of gyrating to *musical songs* about *pure virgins* (i.e., *one hundred percent pure*), all the while enjoying an *upward trajectory*—rather than a *downward descent*—of *positive earnings.* "Can even *one single person,*" she asked, "turn my otherwise *scary nightmare* into a *fairytale story* by helping to pay the *tuition cost* of my *retooling and retraining* once I become an *undergraduate student?*"

As I listened closely to her words, I *actually experienced* an *important breakthrough* in my *ongoing and continual* search to find my true *connecting link* with the *modern world of today.* For the first time, I felt the *driving force* that could lead me to my *preordained destiny,* satisfy my *unrealized potential,* and fulfill my hope of achieving *even balance* in my life. What I had to do was *crystal clear:* I would help all people—even the *lowly down-trodden*—end their *habitual addiction* to *repetitious tautologies.* In *incremental stages,* beginning with this *unique and one-of-a-kind* book, I would dedicate myself to exposing *specific examples* of tautological abuse and eradicating them from our *planet Earth.*

❧ Acknowledgments ❧

T his book grew and matured because it was nurtured by family, friends, and dedicated editors.

I am indebted to Jim Goodwin and Darla Anderson for contributing numerous tautologies and offering editorial insights that improved the text; Rmax Goodwin, Dan Kallan, and Dylan Cooper for energetically bringing additional entries to my attention; scores of students who joined the hunt, even if I did give them extra credit for their efforts; and Linda Kallan for continually reminding me to choose carefully from the tautological bounty I had amassed since I began writing this book in 1991.

Wayne Rowe and Yvonne Lenard believed in the work and introduced it to Mike Larsen and Elizabeth Pomada, literary agents, who would represent and advise me well. I am also grateful to Neal Kallan, who viewed the project with the kind of enthusiasm every author needs. I especially want to thank my editor, Alice van Straalen, for her perceptive analysis and guidance.

I would be remiss if I did not recognize the legion of writers and speakers who throughout the years unwittingly supplied me with hundreds of tautologies. None of you must rest on your laurels. Indeed, without your continued participation there can be no second edition of *Armed Gunmen, True Facts, and Other Ridiculous Nonsense.*

A Complete List
of All Listings

consensus of opinion,
108
constantly evolving, 106
continue to persist, 106
continue to remain, 106
continuously without
interruption, 106
contributing factor, 102
converge together, 82
conversational dialogue,
77
convicted felon, 9
cooperate together, 82
core essence, 67
correspond back and
forth, 90
cover over, 47
crazy lunatic, 5
crumble apart, 89
crystal clear, 129
cubic feet in volume, 110
curious in nature, 110
current fad, 117
current trend, 117
currently in progress,
106
curved arc, 112

D

damp fog, 127
dangerous lightning, 9
DC current, 102

dead body, 12
dead corpse, 12
deadly killer, 12
decapitate the head, 19
deceitful lie, 3
deceptive lie, 3
deliberate lie, 3
deliberately on purpose,
128
depreciate in value, 110
descend down, 40
different varieties, 113
difficult dilemma, 18
disappear from sight, 39
disappear from view, 39
disclose for the first
time, 84
disintegrate into pieces,
89
disorganized mess, 7
divided by a partition,
89
divulge for the first time,
84
DL list, 102
DMZ zone, 102
DOS operating system,
102
dot.com, 102
down in the basement,
64
downward descent, 128
dressed in clothes, 110
drink down, 41

driving force, 128
drop down, 41
drunken sot, 6
dumb mute, 25
duplicate copy, 65
DVD disk, 102
dwindle down, 41

E

each and every, 68
earlier in time, 110
Easter Sunday, 58
either one, 115
either one or the other,
115
electrical voltage, 5
eliminate out, 107
emerge out, 115
emergency situation,
128
empty hole, 109
empty vacuum, 109
end product, 72
end result, 72
endorse the back, 92
enter in, 45
enter into, 115
equal halves, 80
ER room, 103
erode away, 39
essential core, 67
essential necessity, 71

essential prerequisite, 71
estimated at about, 69
even balance, 129
evening soiree, 117
evening sunset, 127
eventually inevitable, 63
exact duplicate, 78
exact equivalent, 78
exact mirror image, 78
exactly identical, 78
exactly the same, 78
excessive verbiage, xi
exit out, 115
expedite quickly, 49
extend out, 115
extra bonus, 82
extreme fanatic, 7

F

face-to-face
    confrontation, 9
factual and accurate, 68
fade away, 39
fair and equitable, 68
fairytale story, 128
fall down, 40
false fabrication, 4
false facade, 4
false front, 4
false illusion, 4
false misrepresentation, 4
false pretense, 4

familiar friend, 21
families with children, 83
famous celebrity, 35
fatally electrocute, 19
farewell swan song, 96
fellow colleague, 28
fellow classmate, 28
fellow peer, 28
few in number, 110
fiery conflagration, 105
fill up, 40
filter out, 107
filthy dirty, 7
final adieu, 117
final climax, 96
final completion, 96
final conclusion, 96
final end, 96
final farewell, 96
final outcome, 96
final upshot, 96
fine mist, 127
first began, 27
first coined, 27
first conceived, 27
first created, 27
first debuted, 27
first discovered, 27
first established, 27
first ever, 27
first founded, 27
first introduced, 27
first invented, 27
first originated, 27

first prototype, 27
first revealed, 27
first started, 27
first uncovered, 27
first unveiled, 27
first-time beginner, 25
flee quickly, 49
fleeting instant, 114
fleeting moment, 114
flock together, 82
flood over, 47
flower boutonniere, 78
follow after, 43
follow behind, 43
foot pedal, 116
forced slavery, 128
forcible rape, 11
forecast ahead, 8
foreign-born immigrant,
    109
foreign import, 109
forewarn, 8
fortunate luck, 72
forward progress, 44
free gift, 119
free giveaway, 119
free of charge, 119
free pass, 119
freezing ice, 105
fresh beginner, 25
frozen tundra, 105
full and complete, 68
full stop, 42
funny comic, 30

readily apparent, 45
real fact, 85
real truth, 85
realization of a dream
    come true, 127
rebound back, 48
recede back, 48
recoil back, 48
reconvert, 107
recur again, 42
recur over and over, 42
recurring motif, 42
recurring pattern, 42
recycled and used again,
    68
red in color, 111
red robin, 23
reduce down, 41
reflect back, 48
regular routine, 127
reiterate again, 42
relic from the past, 116
remaining residue, 99
remand back, 48
remit back, 48
remove and eliminate,
    xi
repay back, 48
repeat again, 42
repeat over, 42
repetitious tautology,
    129
repetitive motif, 42
repetitive pattern, 42

repetitive redundancy,
    xi
reply back, 48
required prerequisite,
    71
reserve ahead, 9
residual trace, 33
respond back, 48
restate again, 42
restore back, 48
resume again, 42
retooling and retraining,
    128
retreat back, 48
return back, 48
return response, 90
reuse again, 42
reveal for the first time,
    84
revert back, 48
revive again, 42
ridiculous nonsense, 15
right-hand side, 58
rise up, 40
roar loudly, 88
rotate around, 50
round cylinder, 50
royal highness, 24
royal king, 24
royal prince, 24
royal princess, 24
royal queen, 24
rural countryside, 58
rural farm, 58

S

sacred scripture, 112
sadly tragic, 128
safe sanctuary, 58
salsa sauce, 127
SALT talks, 103
SAM missile, 103
SAT test, 103
scary nightmare, 128
scheduled appointment,
    63
scream loudly, 88
scrubbed clean, 7
seasoned veteran, 25
see with their own two
    eyes, xi
seesaw up and down, 90
self-confessed, 16
self-portrait of myself, 16
separate and discrete, 68
separate apart, 89
serious crisis, 17
sever off, 89
shape and form, 68
shared dialogue, 77
shout loudly, 88
shriek loudly, 88
shrimp scampi, 127
shrink down, 41
shuttle back and forth, 90
sick leave time, 60
simply plain, 112
singing duet, 31

various and sundry, 68
various varieties, 113
VAT tax, 103
VIN number, 103
violent explosion, 7
visible to the eye, 111
visual sight, 124
vital necessity, 17
volley back and forth,
    90

W

waffle back and forth,
    90
warn ahead, 9
was the former, 92
wealthy millionaire, 31
wealthy philanthropist,
    31

weave in and out, 45
weave together, 82
weird freak, 16
well-established custom,
    72
well-established norm,
    72
well-established
    protocol, 72
well-established
    standard, 72
well-established track
    record, 73
well-established
    tradition, 73
whether or not, 89
while at the same time,
    60
wide-mouthed grin,
    105
widow of the late, 33

wild savage, 17
windy outside, 59
wise sage, 31
with au jus, 117
wooden stick, 123
worthy of merit, 111
written document, 121
written script, 121

Y

yell and scream, 68
yell loudly, 88
yet however, 91
yet nevertheless, 91
young adolescent, 35
young baby, 35
young infant, 35
young juvenile, 35
young lad, 35

This book features reproductions of engravings by George Cruikshank, perhaps the best English illustrator of the nineteenth century.

For seventy years, Cruikshank's work appeared in advertisements, newspapers, magazines, and books. He is most celebrated for his illustrations of Charles Dickens's novels.

Cruikshank's work was reproduced from these sources:

John Buchanan-Brown, *The Book Illustrations of George Cruikshank.* Charles E. Tuttle Company, 1980.

Hilary and Mary Evans, *The Life and Art of George Cruikshank 1792–1878.* S. G. Phillips, Inc., 1978.

Humorous Illustrations by George Cruikshank. Simpkin, Marshall, Hamilton, Kent & Co., n.d.

Richard A. Vogler, *Graphic Works of George Cruikshank.* Dover Publications, Inc., 1979.

ABOUT THE AUTHOR

Richard Kallan received his Ph.D. in communication studies from Northwestern University. He has taught writing and speaking courses for more than thirty years, most recently for the University of Southern California; the University of California, Santa Barbara; and California State Polytechnic University, Pomona, where he chairs the Department of Communication. In addition, he works with businesses, corporations, and government agencies by offering on-site workshops on business writing and professional speaking.

Kallan is the coauthor of *How to Take the Fog Out of Business Writing* (Dartnell, 1994) and has published scholarly articles in such journals as *Communication Monographs, Journalism Quarterly,* and *Journal of Popular Culture.* He has lived in Santa Barbara, California, since 1989.

A NOTE ON THE TYPE

This book was set in Monotype Dante, a typeface designed by Giovanni Mardersteig (1892–1977). Conceived as a private type for the Officina Bodoni in Verona, Italy, Dante was originally cut only for hand composition by Charles Malin, the famous Parisian punch cutter, between 1946 and 1952. Its first use was in an edition of Boccaccio's *Trattatello in laude di Dante* that appeared in 1954. The Monotype Corporation's version of Dante followed in 1957. Although modeled on the Aldine type used for Pietro Cardinal Bembo's treatise *De Aetna* in 1495, Dante is a thoroughly modern interpretation of the venerable face.

Composed by North Market Street Graphics,
Lancaster, Pennsylvania
Printed and bound by R. R. Donnelley and Sons,
Crawfordsville, Indiana
Designed by Virginia Tan